Introduction to Conservation of Indian Monuments

By Siva Prasad Bose and Joy Bose

Contents

Dedication

This book is dedicated to all those who have been involved in the conservation of the ancient archeological heritage of India.

Preface

India has a rich history worthy of preservation. The number of temples, mosques, tombs, ancient city ruins, palaces and other monuments, is staggering in India. Even today, archeologists are finding ruins of great monuments in remote and not so remote locations.

Sadly, various factors such as development, erosion etc. have caused and are causing damage to our ancient heritage. Unplanned expansions of cities, building of new roads and shopping malls and residential areas, unrestricted tourism, all often end up eroding what is left of our archeological heritage.

In this book we introduce to the reader some concepts related to preservation of ancient buildings and monuments. We discuss about the archeological survey of India, its history and objectives. We introduce world agreements such as the Venice Charter and Burra charter that relate to the principles for preservation of heritage. Then we go through some of the actual preservation and restoration techniques, showing their application in preserving and restoring some famous monuments and not so famous monuments.

It is hoped that this book will provide the interested reader with useful information about the concepts and techniques of preservation. This edition also covers newer topics such as the role of digital technologies including 3D scanning, LiDAR, and artificial intelligence in modern conservation work, as well as the growing challenge of climate change to India's built heritage, and India's expanding role in international heritage conservation in Southeast Asia and beyond.

Acknowledgements

In preparing this book, the authors would like to acknowledge help from the following sources:

- AK Seshadri. Conservation of Monuments in India. Book India Publishing Co, Delhi.
- G Thomson (Eds.) Recent Advances in Conservation. Butterworths.
- CPWD, Government of India. Conservation of Heritage Buildings: A Guide.
- National Policy for Conservation of the Ancient Monuments, Archeological Sites and Remains.
- Batra, N. L. (1996). Heritage Conservation: Preservation and restoration of monuments. Aryan Books International
- Custodians of the past: 150 years of the Archaeological Survey of India by Gautam Sengupta (editor); Abha Narain Lambah (editor). Archaeological Survey of India, Ministry of Culture, Government of India, 2012
- ICOMOS Australia. The Burra charter. 2013
- NPTEL course on Architectural Conservation And Historic Preservation By Prof. Sanghamitra Basu, IIT Kharagpur.

- Archaeological Survey of India. National Conservation Policy, 2014. Ministry of Culture, Government of India.
- ICOMOS. The Nara Document on Authenticity. ICOMOS, 1994.
- Vivekananda International Foundation. India's Role in the Conservation of Cultural Heritage in Southeast Asia. July 2024.

- Press Information Bureau, Government of India. Measures to Preserve Cultural Sites from the Adverse Impact of Environment. 2024.

Note: Unless indicated, photos of the historical sites (that are not taken from Wikimedia) were taken personally by the authors.

Chapter 1: Introduction to Principles of Conservation

In this chapter we discuss some of the principles of conservation of ancient monuments.

India has a huge cultural heritage and a number of historical ancient, medieval and even modern monuments worthy of conservation. These include religious buildings such as temples, mosques and churches, secular residential buildings such as palaces and havelis, as well as military cum residential buildings such as forts. Such monuments inspire the people and give us a sense of awe of our ancient history and the architectural genius of our ancestors and the various cultures that constitute India today.

Many of these buildings are sadly under varying states of decay or neglect, for various reasons including lack of funds and ill-planned development.

1.1 Meaning of Conservation and its activities

The word conservation is a general term that is widely used in the context of preservation of old monuments. It generally means the actions taken to prevent decay and damage to the monuments. It includes all related actions aimed towards the preservation of our cultural heritage.

As per the Burra charter, Cultural significance means aesthetic, historic, scientific, social or spiritual value for past, present or future generations. Conservation means all the processes of looking after a place so as to retain its cultural significance.

Generally, conservation includes the following activities: preservation, consolidation, restoration, reconstruction, transplantation and protection of the ecology and environment around the building or site. In the following sections, we discuss each of these in detail.

1.2 Preservation

Preservation refers to day to day actions taken to preserve and maintain a monument in its current location, such as by keeping it clean and protecting it from vandalism. It also includes actions taken to prevent harm to the monument such as cutting of growing vegetation that damages the structure of the monument, prevention of seepage of water such as leaking rainwater from the roofs and walls.

As per the Burra Charter, preservation is taken to mean "Maintaining a place in its existing state and preventing further deterioration". As per the National Policy for Conservation of ancient monuments and archeological sites protected by Archeological Survey of India (ASI), preservation should be the major objective in the case of monuments with high archaeological value. These are the archaeological sites or remains of a monument or portions of monuments with decorative features, including those with applied ornamentation, such as wall paintings, inscriptions and calligraphy, sculptures, etc.

Some examples of preservation done by ASI on sites in India include the following: In the Taj Mahal in Agra, the ASI employed chemical treatments to remove damage and de-coloration of the monument due to pollution from the nearby industrial areas. In the Elephanta caves in Mumbai, ASI performed stabilization of the rock and conservation of the sculptures in the various caves.

1.3 Consolidation

Consolidation refers to actions taken to improve or replace damaged or deteriorated parts of monuments in their current locations. The objective is to preserve its structural integrity and also its aesthetics. It can include things such as grouting of the monuments, injection of cement or adhesive materials to secure wall paintings and similar acts of consolidation.

Examples of consolidation done by ASI in India include the following: In the Taj Mahal in Agra, ASI performed cleaning and restoration work to preserve its marble surfaces and intricate carvings. In the Red Fort in Delhi, ASI did work to repair the walls. In the Konark Sun Temple in Odisha, work was done to preserve the structural integrity in early 20th century, by putting sand and stones in the main hall and sealing the inside of the main building from visitors.

1.4 Restoration

Restoration includes actions taken for repairing and restoring the missing or decayed portions of the monuments so as to resemble the surviving portions, and maintain their original form and condition. The team doing the restoration should have access to necessary historical knowledge of research about the original materials and techniques used for constructing the monument. They should, as much as possible, use similar materials and techniques as the original while doing the restoration. As per the Burra charter, restoration is defined as "Returning a place to a known earlier state by removing accretions or by reassembling existing elements without the introduction of new material." Modern techniques such as 3D reconstruction of monuments and 3D printing can be used as tools to better and more accurately restore the monument to its former shape.

As per the National Policy for Conservation of ancient monuments and archeological sites protected by ASI, restoration may be undertaken on monuments with high architectural value and only in parts of a monument wherein there are missing geometric or floral patterns, or structural members of a monument which have been damaged recently.

At no cost, shall an attempt to restore an entire building be allowed as it will falsify history and will compromise its authenticity. Similarly, decorative features such as wall paintings, inscriptions, calligraphy and sculptures should also not be restored.

Examples of restoration done by ASI on ancient monuments and sites include: Restoration work performed by ASI In the Ajanta caves in Mumbai to preserve the sculptures and carvings. In the Sanchi Stupa, a famous Buddhist stupa in Madhya Pradesh, restoration work has been done to preserve the stupa and the carvings and sculptures.

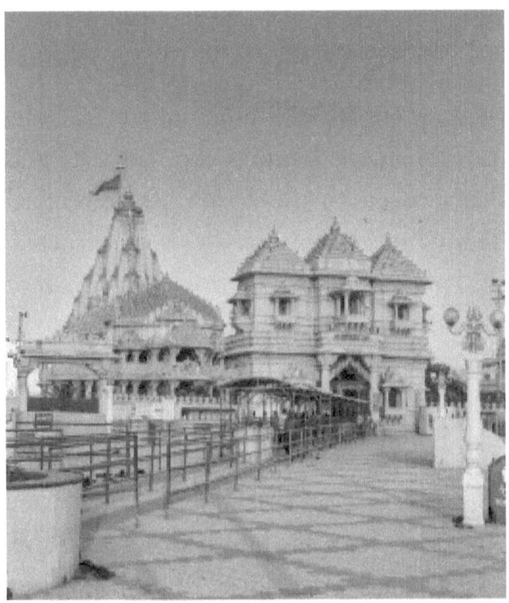

Figure: Somnath temple in Gujarat, rebuilt after independence. Ms Sarah Welch, CC BY-SA 4.0 <https://creativecommons.org/licenses/by-sa/4.0>, via Wikimedia Commons

1.5 Reconstruction

As per the Burra charter, reconstruction is defined as "Returning a place to a known if there is sufficient evidence. and is distinguished from restoration by the introduction of new material."

As per the National Policy for Conservation of ancient monuments and archeological sites protected by ASI, reconstruction may be undertaken for such monuments wherein such an intervention is the only way by which to retain or retrieve their integrity / context and without which its survival is impossible. Reconstruction should be attempted only in extreme cases, such as damage or destruction due to the impact of a disaster (natural or human induced) or structural failure, and should be undertaken only on the basis of evidence and not conjecture.

Some examples of reconstruction on ancient monuments in India include the following: The Somnath Temple in Gujarat was reconstructed after independence based on the design of the original temple. The Vijaya Vittala Temple in Hampi was also reconstructed, with some parts such as damaged pillars and smaller shrines being part of the reconstruction.

1.6 Transplantation

Transplantation refers to actions taken for the removal of the monument, in some cases brick by brick, and rebuilding of the same monument with the same or similar materials but at a different site, without changing its character and originality. These salvaging operations have resulted in saving several monuments from destruction and saving them for posterity. Transplantation of a monument is usually performed in case of a need, such as when a dam, road or building is being constructed on the site and which endangers its existence. It can also be needed when the structural integrity of the site is threatened because of any reason, and so the monument must be transplanted to save it.

As per the National Policy for conservation, transplantation or translocation of a monument is to be done only in the rarest of rare circumstances, and that it should only be undertaken as a means for safeguarding the integrity of the monument.

An example is the transplantation of the Nagarjunakonda remains by archeologists and reconstructing them on a nearby hill which became an island, before they were submerged by the Nagarjunasagar dam in the 1960s.

1.7 Protection of Environment and Ecology

While doing activities for conservation of monuments, it is also important to pay attention to aspects of the ecology and the environment around the monument and preserve them also from destruction. This can include things such as trees and water bodies and even wildlife and birds that live around the monument. Environmental pollution around a monument or site, for example, can damage the monument significantly and so must be prevented.

An example of protection of environment and ecology around heritage monuments in India is the case of the Taj Mahal in Agra. Since Taj Mahal was facing huge pollution problems from nearby factories and industrial zone in Agra, the Supreme court of India ordered to close down the polluting industries and create a mandatory pollution free zone around the Taj Mahal.

1.8 Factors that cause destruction in monuments over the years

Some of the factors that cause destruction and decay of monuments with time are as follows:

Atmospheric decay: This may be due to constant exposure to the elements of the atmosphere such as sun and rain.

Atmospheric pollution: This can damage monuments in areas where the industrial pollution or pollution from vehicle emissions releases effluents in the air, which damage the buildings in the vicinity.

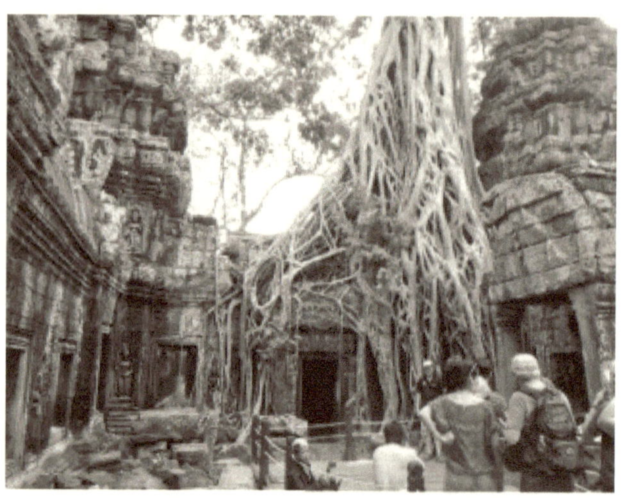

Figure: Roots of a tree on the buildings of the famous Ta Prohm (Brahma) temple in Cambodia. Photo taken by author.

Roots of vegetation: Trees may have over the years embedded their roots in the walls of the monuments, causing them untold damage. This often occurs in the walls of the building as well as elevated structures like gopurams of temples and domes of mosques. The cavities of the buildings slowly get filled up with dust and drops of water, which becomes manure with time. Seeds of trees like neem and other plants, dropped by birds, then grow into trees in this manure soil in the cavities of the building. This causes further damage to the building as the trees expand the cavities while growing, causing cracks in the walls and other parts. This damage due to roots of trees can be seen in the famous Ta Prohm Hindu temple in Seam Reap in Cambodia. Therefore, any vegetation growing on the building should be cut down to conserve it.

Weathering: Gradation of weathering happens of the roof and walls of the monuments, which are exposed to constant sun and rain.

Water: Water stagnates inside the monuments, often due to blockages in the drainage system of the monument.

Humidity: Humidity can also play a role in damaging ancient monuments, often when accompanied by lack of maintenance.

Changes in environment and ecology: This can further cause the monuments to be damaged.

Lack of maintenance and human neglect: Due to neglect, moss, molasses and lichen may grow on the walls of the monument over time, significantly damaging the outer structure by damaging the top layers of stone and bricks and exposing the inner core of the monument. Similarly, cobwebs can form in only a few days, along with accumulation of dust and vegetation. Therefore, regular maintenance and cleaning of ancient buildings should be performed.

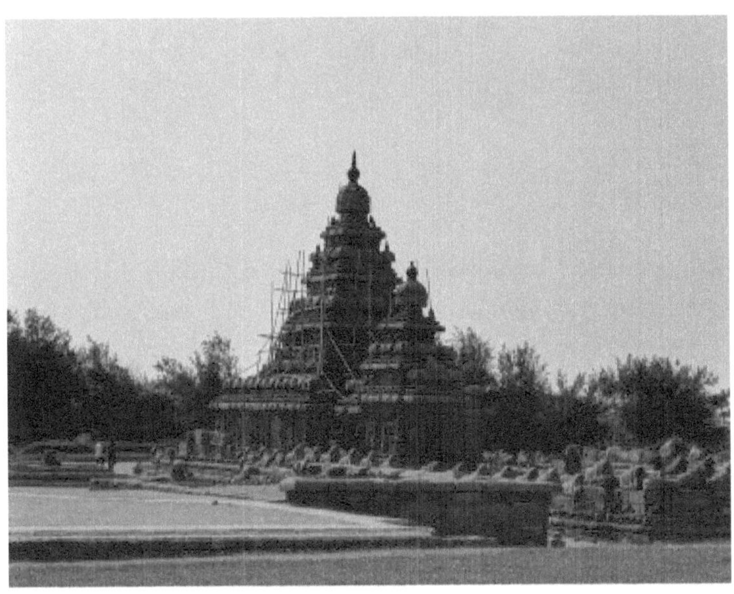

Figure: The shore temple complex in Mahabalipuram, which is partly weathered due to seawater. Photo taken by author.

Saline action: Monuments located close to the sea-coast may be damaged by salty sea water. The stones or bricks making the monument may get weakened by the sea water over time. An example of this can be seen in the shore temple in Mahabalipuram, Tamil Nadu which was located at the sea coast: one can see that the sculptures of the temple have been weathered. To protect such monuments, a wall of gravel stones should be erected around the endangered monuments close to the sea.

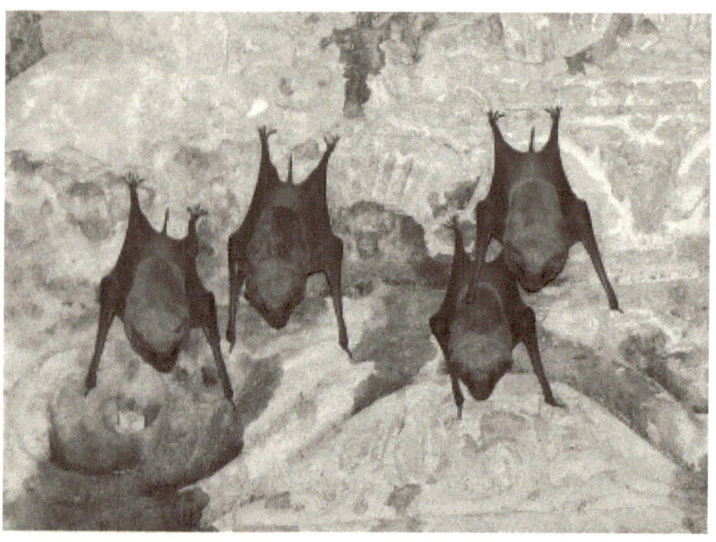

Figure: Bats in the sun temple at Modhera. Bernard Gagnon, CC BY-SA 3.0 <https://creativecommons.org/licenses/by-sa/3.0>, via Wikimedia Commons

Nuisance of animals and bats: This can seriously injure the monuments, partly through the urine and excreta of animals that causes accumulation of ground salts that damage the monuments. In many old Indian temples, the stench of bats living inside is a common occurrence. To conserve the monuments, such animals and bats should be driven out and netting should be put on the windows and other openings of the monuments.

Natural disasters: Earthquakes, hurricanes, lightning, thunder, strong winds all can play a role in damaging the monuments over time. Even natural forces like gravity can, over time, cause the building to collapse. For example, the upper part of the Qutub minar in Delhi was damaged by an earthquake in 1803.

Increase or decrease of the ground water levels: This too can cause damage to the stability of the monuments.

Vandalism: This is a human caused major destructive factor that can lead to wholesale or partial destruction of the monuments via mutilation, writing on walls, spraying graffiti, defacing and so on. A lot of the important historical sites in India have fallen prey to vandalism. This can also include historical acts of vandalism by external invaders, such as the destruction of the temple of Somnath by Mahmud of Ghazni in the 11th century.

Thefts: Thefts of artifacts from historical monuments is another big problem in India. Things such as statues of deities, particularly temple bronzes and other sculptures can fetch a very good price in the national or international markets, especially in international auctions. This kind of theft is often done by organized gangs operating internationally. India has a rich treasure of cultural heritage combined with lax security for many important monuments, resulting in it being a prime target for thief gangs. It can also include simple theft of building materials from the monuments.

1.9 Organizations and guidelines devoted to conservation in India

There are a few organizations that are devoted to the preservation of culture and heritage buildings. Some of these include the following:

- **Archeological Survey of India (ASI)**: This was established during British rule and has an illustrious history in restoring, rescuing and conserving many important monuments in the Indian subcontinent in the past century or more.
- **Indian National Trust for Art and Cultural Heritage (INTACH)** which is the largest conservation related non-governmental organization in India is also involved in conservation efforts at different levels.
- Many other organizations are also involved in preservation. In particular, the **Aga Khan Trust for Culture (AKTC)** is also involved in funding the preservation of many monuments such as Qutub Shahi tomb in Hyderabad.

There are also guidelines for conservation from international bodies such as the following:

- **Venice Charter** (Short for International Charter for the conservation and Restoration of Monuments and Sites) adopted in 1964.
- **UNESCO Convention Concerning the Protection of the World Cultural and Natural Heritage** Adopted by the General Conference at its seventeenth session Paris, 16 November 1972
- **Burra Charter**, Australia ICOMOS Charter for Places of Cultural Significance. Published in Australia in 1979.

1.10 Conclusion

In this chapter, we have discussed the meaning and factors of conservation and some of the factors that cause damage and destruction of monuments.

Chapter 2: International Agreements for Conservation of Monuments

In this chapter, we discuss two important international agreements related to conservation of monuments, namely the Venice Charter and Burra Charter. In particular, the principals described in the Venice Charter of 1964 is regarded as a model for conservation of monuments over the world.

2.1 Venice Charter of 1964

The Venice charter comprises a set of guidelines drawn by a group of experts in 1964 for the conservation and restoration of historic monuments. It is an influential document which has become the standard document for conservation all over the world.

Text of the Venice Charter: Taken from https://www.icomos.org/en/participer/179-articles-en-francais/ressources/chartes-and-standards/157-thevenice-charter

The IInd International Congress of Architects and Technicians of Historic Monuments, which met in Venice in 1964, approved the following text:

Article 1. The concept of a historic monument embraces not only the single architectural work but also the urban or rural setting in which is found the evidence of a particular civilization, a significant development or a historic event. This applies not only to great works of art but also to more modest works of the past which have acquired cultural significance with the passing of time.

Article 2. The conservation and restoration of monuments must have recourse to all the sciences and techniques which can contribute to the study and safeguarding of the architectural heritage.

Article 3. The intention in conserving and restoring monuments is to safeguard them no less as works of art than as historical evidence.

CONSERVATION

Article 4. It is essential to the conservation of monuments that they be maintained on a permanent basis.

Article 5. The conservation of monuments is always facilitated by making use of them for some socially useful purpose. Such use is therefore desirable but it must not change the lay-out or decoration of the building. It is within these limits only that modifications demanded by a change of function should be envisaged and may be permitted.

Article 6. The conservation of a monument implies preserving a setting which is not out of scale. Wherever the traditional setting exists, it must be kept. No new construction, demolition or modification which would alter the relations of mass and colour must be allowed.

Article 7. A monument is inseparable from the history to which it bears witness and from the setting in which it occurs. The moving of all or part of a monument cannot be allowed except where the safeguarding of that monument demands it or where it is justified by national or international interest of paramount importance.

Article 8. Items of sculpture, painting or decoration which form an integral part of a monument may only be removed from it if this is the sole means of ensuring their preservation.

RESTORATION

Article 9. The process of restoration is a highly specialized operation. Its aim is to preserve and reveal the aesthetic and historic value of the monument and is based on respect for original material and authentic documents. It must stop at the point where conjecture begins, and in this case moreover any extra work which is indispensable must be distinct from the architectural composition and must bear a contemporary stamp. The restoration in any case must be preceded and followed by an archaeological and historical study of the monument.

Article 10. Where traditional techniques prove inadequate, the consolidation of a monument can be achieved by the use of any modern technique for conservation and construction, the efficacy of which has been shown by scientific data and proved by experience.

Article 11. The valid contributions of all periods to the building of a monument must be respected, since unity of style is not the aim of a restoration. When a building includes the superimposed work of different periods, the revealing of the underlying state can only be justified in exceptional circumstances and when what is removed is of little interest and the material which is brought to light is of great historical, archaeological or aesthetic value, and its state of preservation good enough to justify the action. Evaluation of the importance of the elements involved and the decision as to what may be destroyed cannot rest solely on the individual in charge of the work.

Article 12. Replacements of missing parts must integrate harmoniously with the whole, but at the same time must be distinguishable from the original so that restoration does not falsify the artistic or historic evidence.

Article 13. Additions cannot be allowed except in so far as they do not detract from the interesting parts of the building, its traditional setting, the balance of its composition and its relation with its surroundings.

HISTORIC SITES

Article 14. The sites of monuments must be the object of special care in order to safeguard their integrity and ensure that they are cleared and presented in a seemly manner. The work of conservation and restoration carried out in such places should be inspired by the principles set forth in the foregoing articles.

EXCAVATIONS

Article 15. Excavations should be carried out in accordance with scientific standards and the recommendation defining international principles to be applied in the case of archaeological excavation adopted by UNESCO in 1956.

Ruins must be maintained and measures necessary for the permanent conservation and protection of architectural features and of objects discovered must be taken. Furthermore, every means must be taken to facilitate the understanding of the monument and to reveal it without ever distorting its meaning.

All reconstruction work should however be ruled out "a priori". Only anastylosis, that is to say, the reassembling of existing but dismembered parts can be permitted. The material used for integration should always be recognizable and its use should be the least that will ensure the conservation of a monument and the reinstatement of its form.

PUBLICATION

Article 16. In all works of preservation, restoration or excavation, there should always be precise documentation in the form of analytical and critical reports, illustrated with drawings and photographs. Every stage of the work of clearing, consolidation, rearrangement and integration, as well as technical and formal features identified during the course of the work, should be included. This record should be placed in the archives of a public institution and made available to research workers. It is recommended that the report should be published.

2.2 UNESCO Convention Concerning the Protection of the World Cultural and Natural Heritage

This convention was regarding the UNESCO World Heritage Sites, a carefully selected list of sites around the world that are culturally or naturally significant and are protected and promoted by UNESCO. The convention was adopted by the General Conference at its seventeenth session in Paris on 16 November 1972. It establishes the criteria for inclusion of a candidate site into the world heritage list, standards for the appointment of the world heritage committee and the criteria related to the world heritage fund.

Some important articles of the convention related specifically to conservation of world heritage monuments are as follows:

Noting that the cultural heritage and the natural heritage are increasingly threatened with destruction not only by the traditional causes of decay, but also by changing social and economic conditions which aggravate the situation with even more formidable phenomena of damage or destruction,

Considering that deterioration or disappearance of any item of the cultural or natural heritage constitutes a harmful impoverishment of the heritage of all the nations of the world, Considering that protection of this heritage at the national level often remains incomplete because of the scale of the resources which it requires and of the insufficient economic, scientific, and technological resources of the country where the property to be protected is situated,

Recalling that the Constitution of the Organization provides that it will maintain, increase, and diffuse knowledge by assuring the conservation and protection of the world's heritage, and recommending to the nations concerned the necessary international conventions,

Considering that the existing international conventions, recommendations and resolutions concerning cultural and natural property demonstrate the importance, for all the peoples of the world, of safeguarding this unique and irreplaceable property, to whatever people it may belong,

Considering that parts of the cultural or natural heritage are of outstanding interest and therefore need to be preserved as part of the world heritage of mankind as a whole,

Considering that, in view of the magnitude and gravity of the new dangers threatening them, it is incumbent on the international community as a whole to participate in the protection of the cultural and natural heritage of outstanding universal value, by the granting of collective assistance which, although not taking the place of action by the State concerned, will serve as an efficient complement thereto,

Considering that it is essential for this purpose to adopt new provisions in the form of a convention establishing an effective system of collective protection of the cultural and natural heritage of outstanding universal value, organized on a permanent basis and in accordance with modern scientific methods,

Having decided, at its sixteenth session, that this question should be made the subject of an international convention, Adopts this sixteenth day of November 1972 this Convention.

Article 1 For the purpose of this Convention, the following shall be considered as "cultural heritage":

monuments: architectural works, works of monumental sculpture and painting, elements or structures of an archaeological nature, inscriptions, cave dwellings and combinations of features, which are of outstanding universal value from the point of view of history, art or science;

groups of buildings: groups of separate or connected buildings which, because of their architecture, their homogeneity or their place in the landscape, are of outstanding universal value from the point of view of history, art or science;

sites: works of man or the combined works of nature and man, and areas including archaeological sites which are of outstanding universal value from the historical, aesthetic, ethnological or anthropological point of view.

2.3 The Burra charter

In 1992 the Australian government passed what is known as the Burra charter, also called Australia ICOMOS Charter for Places of Cultural Significance. It has been renewed regularly. It states the principles to be followed in the conservation and preservation of monuments. It was originally inspired by the Venice Charter of 1964 but has a wider scope in that it provides guidelines for conservation of monuments and also considers conservation of non-physical and intangible forms of heritage.

https://australia.icomos.org/wp-content/uploads/The-Burra-Charter-2013-Adopted-31.10.2013.pdf

Articles of the charter mentions the following conservation principles:

Article 2. Conservation and management

2.1 Places of cultural significance should be conserved.

2.2 The aim of conservation is to retain the cultural significance of a place.

2.3 Conservation is an integral part of good management of places of cultural significance.

2.4 Places of cultural significance should be safeguarded and not put at risk or left in a vulnerable state.

Article 3. Cautious approach

3.1 Conservation is based on a respect for the existing fabric, use, associations and meanings. It requires a cautious approach of changing as much as necessary but as little as possible.

3.2 Changes to a place should not distort the physical or other evidence it provides, nor be based on conjecture.

Article 4. Knowledge, skills and techniques

4.1 Conservation should make use of all the knowledge, skills and disciplines which can contribute to the study and care of the place.

4.2 Traditional techniques and materials are preferred for the conservation of significant fabric. In some circumstances modern techniques and materials which offer substantial conservation benefits may be appropriate.

Article 5. Values

5.1 Conservation of a place should identify and take into consideration all aspects of cultural and natural significance without unwarranted emphasis on any one value at the expense of others.

5.2 Relative degrees of cultural significance may lead to different conservation actions at a place.

Article 6. Burra Charter Process

6.1 The cultural significance of a place and other issues affecting its future are best understood by a sequence of collecting and analysing information before making decisions. Understanding cultural significance comes first, then development of policy and finally management of the place in accordance with the policy. This is the Burra Charter Process.

6.2 Policy for managing a place must be based on an understanding of its cultural significance.

6.3 Policy development should also include consideration of other factors affecting the future of a place such as the owner's needs, resources, external constraints and its physical condition.

6.4 In developing an effective policy, different ways to retain cultural significance and address other factors may need to be explored.

6.5 Changes in circumstances, or new information or perspectives, may require reiteration of part or all of the Burra Charter Process.

Article 7. Use

7.1 Where the use of a place is of cultural significance it should be retained.

7.2 A place should have a compatible use

Article 8. Setting

Conservation requires the retention of an appropriate setting. This includes retention of the visual and sensory setting, as well as the retention of spiritual and other cultural relationships that contribute to the cultural significance of the place. New construction, demolition, intrusions or other changes which would adversely affect the setting or relationships are not appropriate.

Article 9. Location

9.1 The physical location of a place is part of its cultural significance. A building, work or other element of a place should remain in its historical location. Relocation is generally unacceptable unless this is the sole practical means of ensuring its survival.

9.2 Some buildings, works or other elements of places were designed to be readily removable or already have a history of relocation. Provided such buildings, works or other elements do not have significant links with their present location, removal may be appropriate.

9.3 If any building, work or other element is moved, it should be moved to an appropriate location and given an appropriate use. Such action should not be to the detriment of any place of cultural significance.

Article 10. Contents

Contents, fixtures and objects which contribute to the cultural significance of a place should be retained at that place. Their removal is unacceptable unless it is: the sole means of ensuring their security and preservation; on a temporary basis for treatment or exhibition; for cultural reasons; for health and safety; or to protect the place. Such contents, fixtures and objects should be returned where circumstances permit and it is culturally appropriate.

Article 11. Related places and objects

The contribution which related places and related objects make to the cultural significance of the place should be retained.

Article 12. Participation

Conservation, interpretation and management of a place should provide for the participation of people for whom the place has significant associations and meanings, or who have social, spiritual or other cultural responsibilities for the place.

Article 13. Co-existence of cultural values

Co-existence of cultural values should always be recognised, respected and encouraged. This is especially important in cases where they conflict.

Article 14. Conservation processes

Conservation may, according to circumstance, include the processes of: retention or reintroduction of a use; retention of associations and meanings; maintenance, preservation, restoration, reconstruction, adaptation and interpretation; and will commonly include a combination of more than one of these. Conservation may also include retention of the contribution that related places and related objects make to the cultural significance of a place.

Article 15. Change

15.1 Change may be necessary to retain cultural significance, but is undesirable where it reduces cultural significance. The amount of change to a place and its use should be guided by the cultural significance of the place and its appropriate interpretation.

Article 16. Maintenance

Maintenance is fundamental to conservation. Maintenance should be undertaken where fabric is of cultural significance and its maintenance is necessary to retain that cultural significance.

Article 17. Preservation

Preservation is appropriate where the existing fabric or its condition constitutes evidence of cultural significance, or where insufficient evidence is available to allow other conservation processes to be carried out.

Article 18. Restoration and reconstruction

Restoration and reconstruction should reveal culturally significant aspects of the place.

Article 19. Restoration

Restoration is appropriate only if there is sufficient evidence of an earlier state of the fabric.

Article 20. Reconstruction

20.1 Reconstruction is appropriate only where a place is incomplete through damage or alteration, and only where there is sufficient evidence to reproduce an earlier state of the fabric. In some cases, reconstruction may also be appropriate as part of a use or practice that retains the cultural significance of the place.

20.2 Reconstruction should be identifiable on close inspection or through additional interpretation.

Article 21. Adaptation

21.1 Adaptation is acceptable only where the adaptation has minimal impact on the cultural significance of the place.

21.2 Adaptation should involve minimal change to significant fabric, achieved only after considering alternatives.

Article 22. New work

22.1 New work such as additions or other changes to the place may be acceptable where it respects and does not distort or obscure the cultural significance of the place, or detract from its interpretation and appreciation.

2.3 The Nara Document on Authenticity (1994)

The Nara Document on Authenticity was adopted in 1994 in Nara, Japan, and represents an important expansion of the principles of the Venice Charter. It was developed as heritage conservation practice spread globally and practitioners began to question whether the authenticity standards embedded in the Venice Charter — which had been developed primarily in the context of European stone monuments — were appropriate for all cultures.

The Nara Document emphasises that judgements about the value of heritage, and the authenticity of its conservation, cannot be made by applying fixed criteria. Instead, it recognises that all cultures have their own legitimate approaches to heritage, determined by their own values, traditions, and technologies. The document explicitly states that it would be impossible to base judgements of value and authenticity within fixed criteria, and calls for respect for all cultural diversity in the world. This is particularly relevant for India, where many religious monuments such as temples are living places of worship that are periodically renewed as part of tradition — a practice that differs from the European model of preserving monuments as they are.

2.4 Delhi Declaration on Heritage and Democracy (2023)

The Delhi Declaration on Heritage and Democracy was adopted at the 19th General Assembly of ICOMOS (International Council on Monuments and Sites) held in New Delhi in December 2023.

ICOMOS is the principal international non-governmental organisation that works for the conservation and protection of cultural heritage places, and is an advisory body to the UNESCO World Heritage Committee. The Delhi Declaration represents a landmark affirmation of the link between heritage conservation and democratic values, recognising that access to cultural heritage is a fundamental human right. It also calls for inclusive participation of local communities in heritage decision-making, moving beyond the idea of heritage as the exclusive domain of specialists. The choice of Delhi as the venue for this declaration underscores India's growing centrality in international heritage discourse.

2.5 Conclusion

In this chapter we have described important international charters and declarations that are used as models for the principles of conservation across the world: the Venice Charter, the UNESCO World Heritage Convention, the Burra Charter, the Nara Document on Authenticity, and the Delhi Declaration on Heritage and Democracy.

Chapter 3: Introduction to the Archeological Survey of India

In this chapter, we discuss the Archeological Survey of India, which is the primary organization dedicated to preservation of heritage monuments in India.

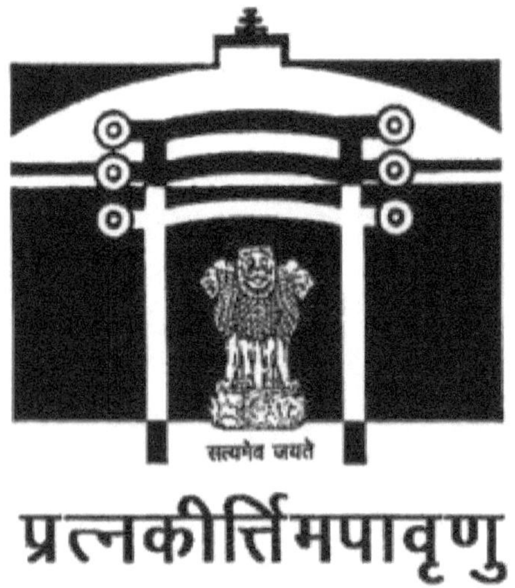

Figure: Logo of Archeological Survey of India. Taken from the Archeological Survey website http://asi.nic.in/

3.1 Origins of the Archeological Survey of India (ASI)

The Archeological Survey of India was established under British rule, mainly to preserve the heritage sites of Indian subcontinent. It has a stellar track record of repairing many of the ancient monuments, discovering new ones through excavations, maintaining the heritage monuments and so on.

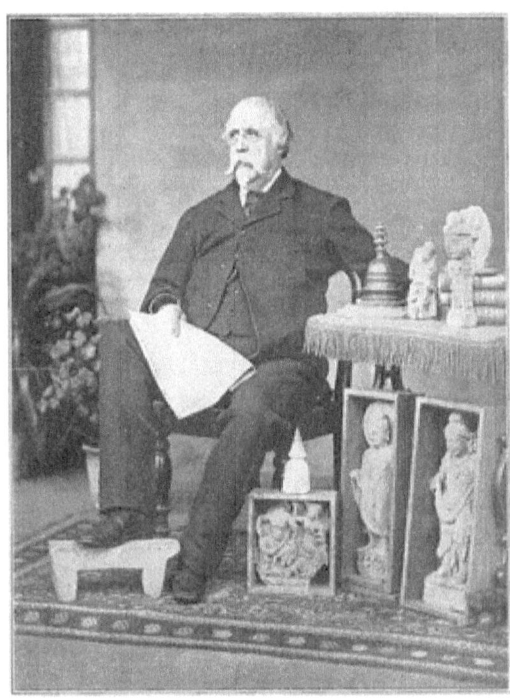

Figure: Sir Alexander Cunningham, first Director General of the Archeological Survey of India. Public domain, via Wikimedia Commons

ASI was founded in 1862 by Alexander Cunningham, who also became its first director general. In the century preceding, the Asiatic society had done stellar service in building interest for Indian culture among the British, starting a trend that ultimately led to the ASI's founding. Many British officials had been instrumental in its promotion. In particular, Lord Curzon, the governor general of India in the beginning of the 1900s, was instrumental in promoting the ASI and strengthening its powers and role in preserving the heritage monuments.

The ASI brought state of the art modern techniques in monument preservation to India and the British also trained many Indian archeologists in such techniques, such as Rakhaldas Banerji, the Indian archeologist who discovered Mohenjodaro.

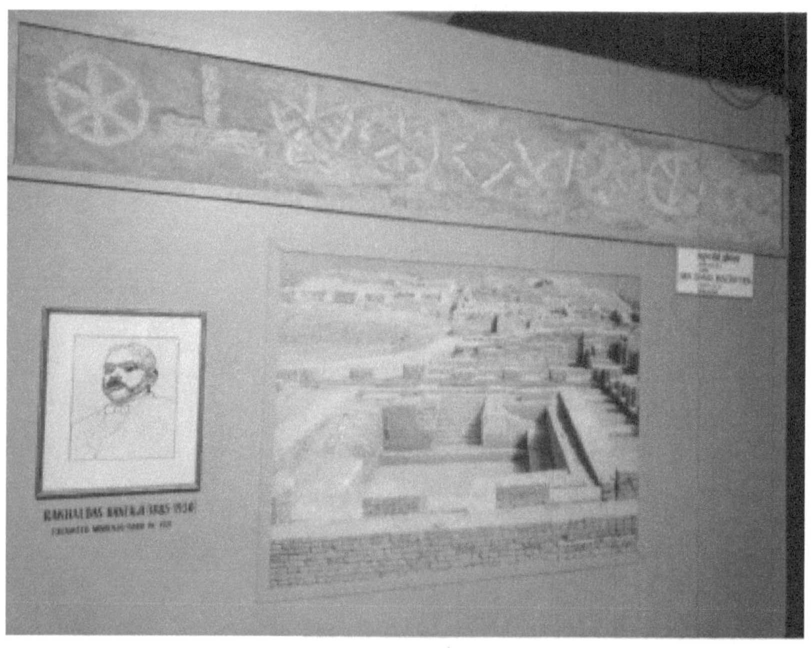

Image: Photo of Rakhaldas Banerji, Indian archeologist who excavated the famous Indus valley site of Mohenjodaro in 1921. National Museum, New Delhi. Photo taken by author.

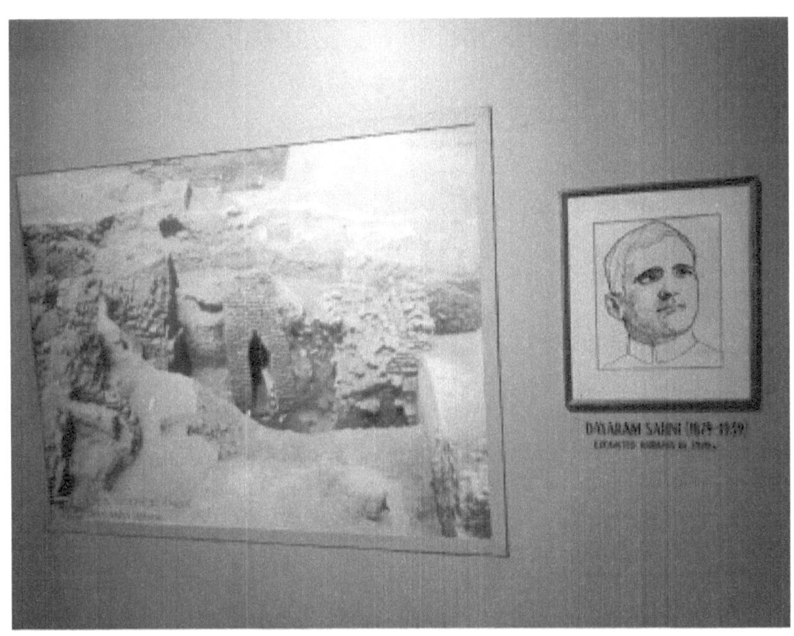

Image: Photo of Dayaram Sahni, Indian archeologist who excavated the famous Indus valley site of Harappa in 1920s. National Museum, New Delhi. Photo taken by author.

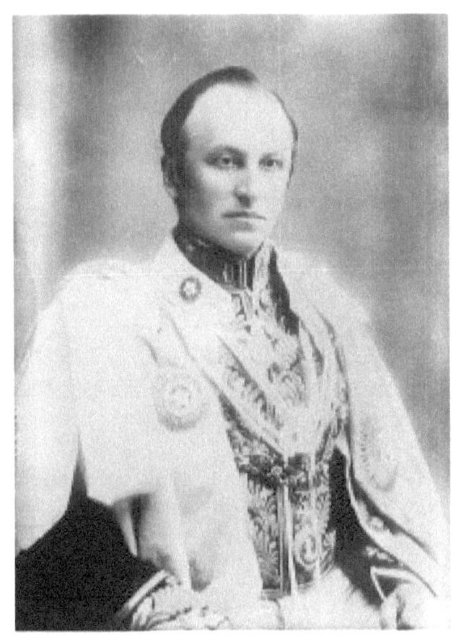

Image: Photo of Lord Curzon, British Viceroy of India from 1899-1905, who played an instrumental role in promoting Archeological Survey of India and its role in protecting important historical sites in the Indian subcontinent. George Grantham Bain Collection (Library of Congress), Public domain, via Wikimedia Commons

3.2 Milestones in the history of ASI

Some of the milestones in the history of the ASI are as follows:

1784 Establishment of the "Asiatic" Society at Calcutta under Sir William Jones

1810 Bengal Resolution XIX, the first attempt to involve the government in intervening through legislation in case of risk to monuments

1847 Delhi Archaeological Society established

1861 Alexander Cunningham appointed as Archaeological Surveyor to the Government of India

1863 Act (XX) promulgated, which vests powers with the government "to prevent injury to and preserve buildings remarkable for their antiquity or for their historical or architectural value"

1871 Government Resolution passed, appointing Alexander Cunningham as the first Director General of the Archaeological Survey

1900 Viceroy Lord Curzon proposes the revival of the post of Director General for the supervision and coordination of the work of the Archaeological Survey of India

1902 John Marshall appointed as Director General of the Archaeological Survey of India

1904 Ancient Monuments Preservation Act passed

1944 Government appoints Sir Mortimer Wheeler as Director General of Archaeological Survey of India

3.3 Objectives of the ASI

The objectives of the archeological survey of India, taken from the ASI website (https://asi.nic.in/about-us/) are as follows:

"The Archaeological Survey of India (ASI), under the Ministry of Culture, is the premier organization for the archaeological researches and protection of the cultural heritage of the nation. Maintenance of ancient monuments and archaeological sites and remains of national importance is the prime concern of the ASI. Besides it regulates all archaeological activities in the country as per the provisions of the Ancient Monuments and Archaeological Sites and Remains Act, 1958. It also regulates Antiquities and Art Treasure Act, 1972."

The ASI has various tasks and objectives including preservation and conservation of heritage monuments, exploring and excavating new archeological sites, running archeological museums, surveys and documentation, training of students and professionals in the area of preservation, publishing books and conducting research on relevant topics and so on. It also manages the world heritage sites in India and other nationally and locally important heritage sites, including facilities for visiting tourists and ticketing etc.

3.4 Principles of Conservation of ASI

The Principles of Conservation of the Archeological Survey of India (from the National Policy for Conservation of ancient monuments and archeological sites protected by ASI, Feb 2014, available at https://asi.nic.in/) are as follows:

1. *The conservation of monuments, archaeological sites and remains constitutes all necessary actions or interventions within and around a monument which are undertaken, as and when deemed necessary, in order to: (a) prolong its life and existence; (b) prevent its damage and deterioration; (c) minimize the impact of external agents of decay (natural and human induced) on its setting, structure and material; and (d) prepare it for natural or human induced disasters.*

2. *A monument or an archaeological site should be subjected to **minimum – whilst only necessary - interventions** so as to maintain its authenticity and integrity. Original / historical material and an architectural / ornamental detail (structural or non-structural) must be valued and retained for as long as possible and should not be replaced without conducting a proper investigation or simply because these have lost their original form and appearance as a result of slight erosion or natural processes of deterioration.*

3. *All efforts to conserve a monument should be made to retain its value and significance, its authenticity and integrity, its visual connections to and from the monument, and to maintain a faithful representation of its original / historic appearance. The purpose of such an effort should be to ensure that the monument is kept in its original state or, in certain cases, restored to an earlier known state or to a state as it was discovered at the time of its identification and notification.*

4. *The conservation of a monument is a continuous process. Adequate resources (human and financial) should be made available to conserve it for posterity.*

5. *Conservation of a monument should, under no circumstance, be based on any conjecture or artistic imagination and should be based on reliable documentary evidences (past conservation records, documents, paintings sketches, drawings, photographs, travelogues, etc.) and/or in situ archaeological evidences.*

6. *Conservation should be treated as a multi-disciplinary enterprise that focuses on developing holistic solutions against various agencies of decay and deterioration that are acting on the monument. Comprehensive and careful study of all relevant aspects should be undertaken to develop an over-arching conservation*

philosophy and approach for each monument.

7. *Conservation of the original / historical material should be aimed as an essential prerequisite to sustain the time-dimension of a monument which confirms its antiquity and faithfully maintains its authenticity.*

8. *Interventions such as restoration, consolidation, reproduction and retrofitting carried out within a monument should, as far as possible, be clearly discernible as a later alteration / repair / restoration, etc., to be able to clearly identify them from the original fabric of the structure. Nonetheless, in certain cases, where a monument is being restored with the intention of merging [a new intervention] with the original fabric, for the sake of maintaining architectural integrity, work must be done very carefully by matching the original material / details in terms of form, color and specification preferably through the use of same material and employing traditional skills as used in the original fabric. Such interventions should, as far as possible, be reversible in nature. The decision for achieving such objectives should be carefully recorded and documented for posterity.*

3.5 Categories of protected monuments under ASI

The various categories of protected monuments under the ASI are as follows:

- Category I World Heritage Sites
- Category II Tentative list of World Heritage Sites
- Category III Identified for inclusion in the World Heritage tentative list
- Category IV Ticketed monuments (other than those mentioned above)
- Category V Identified for categorization as ticketed monuments
- Category VI Living monuments which receive large number of visitors/pilgrims
- Category VII Other monuments located in the Urban/semi

urban limits and in the remote villages

- Category VIII Other category as the Authority may deem fit

3.6 Recent Developments in the ASI

Several important developments at the ASI in recent years reflect a renewed emphasis on technology, public-private partnerships, and international engagement in heritage conservation.

Adopt a Heritage 2.0: Launched in 2023, the Adopt a Heritage 2.0 programme is a public-private partnership initiative designed to foster collaboration between the ASI and corporate stakeholders for the upkeep and promotion of heritage monuments. Under the programme, public sector companies and select private businesses — known as "Monument Mitras" — adopt monuments and are responsible for providing and maintaining basic amenities including drinking water, ease of access, surveillance systems, and tourist facilitation centres. The programme uses corporate social responsibility (CSR) funds, and there is no financial bidding involved. In March 2024, ASI signed Memorandums of Understanding with various agencies formalising the adoption of several significant monuments under this scheme. This model of private participation in publicly managed heritage marks an important new direction in Indian conservation policy.

Budget and Scale: The revenue allocated for preservation of monuments under the ASI has grown significantly, increasing by about 70% over recent years. In 2020-21, the allocation was Rs. 260.90 crores, while in 2023-24 both allocation and expenditure rose to Rs. 443.53 crores. The ASI currently protects and maintains 3,698 centrally protected monuments and sites. Every year, more than 800 monuments are identified for special structural repairs based on assessment by field offices. Excavation funding has also more than doubled, from Rs. 6.53 crore in 2014-15 to Rs. 15 crore in 2024-25.

Hosting the UNESCO World Heritage Committee: India hosted the 46th session of the UNESCO World Heritage Committee at Bharat Mandapam in New Delhi in July 2024. As custodian of 43 World Heritage Sites (as of 2024, with Charaideo Moidams in Assam being the most recently inscribed), India's hosting of this prestigious session reflected the country's growing standing in global heritage conservation. India also signed a cultural property agreement with the United States in 2024 to prevent the illegal trade of cultural property and facilitate the repatriation of stolen antiquities.

3.7 Conclusion

In this chapter we have briefly discussed the Archaeological Survey of India, its history, principles of conservation, recent developments, and its growing role in international heritage preservation.

Chapter 4: Introduction to Indian National Trust for Art and Cultural Heritage

In this chapter, we discuss Indian National Trust for Art and Cultural Heritage (INTACH), which is a non-profit organization dedicated to preservation of unprotected monuments in India.

4.1 What is INTACH

INTACH is a charitable organization registered under the societies act. It was founded in 1984 in Delhi. Its objective is to focus on the preservation of unprotected monuments and cultural items in India and generally spread awareness of heritage and culture among the public. It is also involved in activism among the public against the destruction of important monuments.

It is the largest conservation related organization in India by number of members.

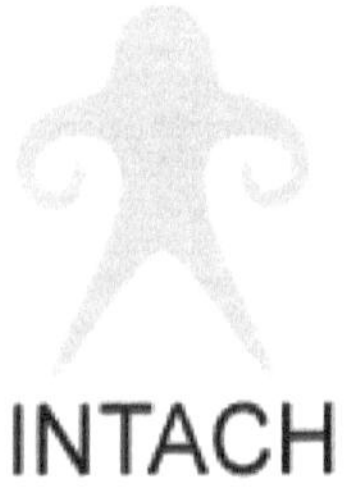

Figure: Logo of INTACH. Taken from http://www.intach.org/

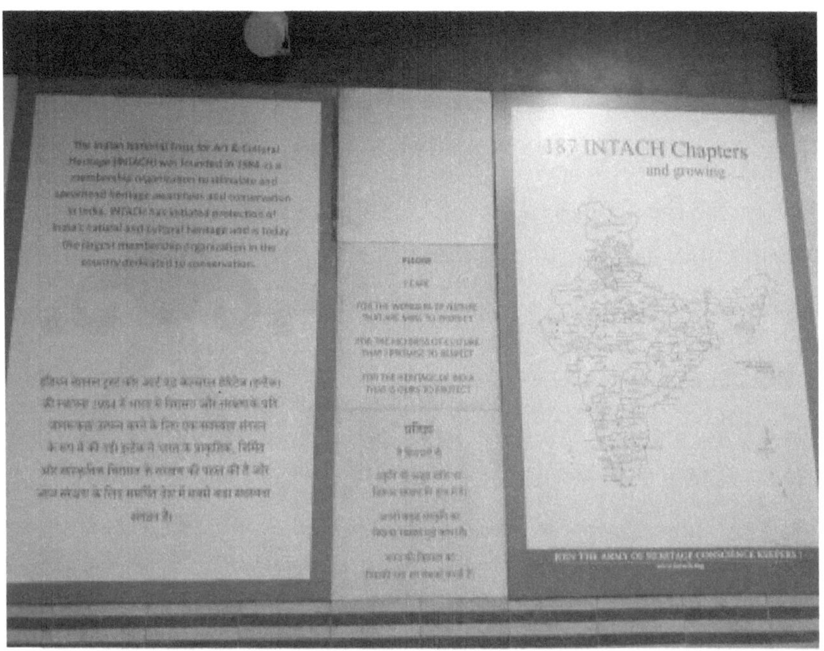

Figure: Poster on INTACH from an exhibition at Jor Bagh Metro station in Delhi. Photo taken by author.

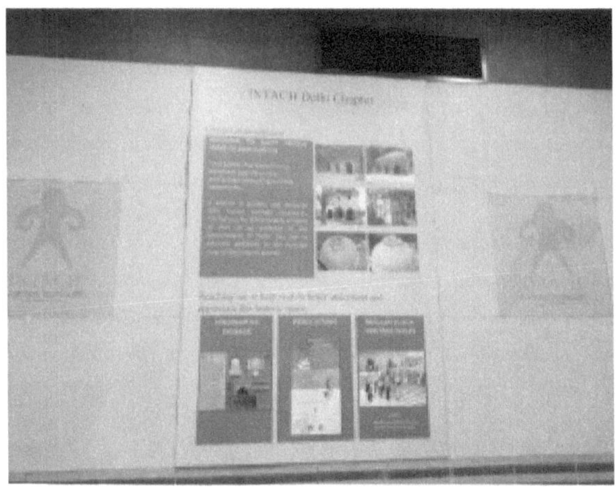

Figure: Poster on INTACH Delhi Chapter from an exhibition at Jor Bagh Metro station in Delhi. Photo taken by author.

4.2 Charter of INTACH

The INTACH charter (taken from the INTACH website http://www.intach.org/about-charter.php) is as follows:

Charter for the Conservation of Unprotected Architectural Heritage and Sites in India

Drawing upon the experience of the Indian National Trust for Art and Cultural Heritage (INTACH) in conserving the unprotected architectural heritage and sites of India within an institutional framework for two decades;

Respecting the invaluable contributions of the Archaeological Survey of India (ASI) and State Departments of Archaeology (SDA) in preserving the finest monuments of India;

Valuing ASI's pioneering role in promoting scientific methods of practice and establishing highest standards of professionalism in preserving monuments; Acknowledging the importance and relevance of principles enunciated in the various International Charters adopted by UNESCO, ICOMOS, et al;

Conscious, however, that a majority of architectural heritage properties and sites in India still remains unidentified, unclassified, and unprotected, thereby subject to attrition on account of neglect, vandalism and insensitive development;

Recognizing the unique resource of the 'living' heritage of Master Builders / Sthapatis / Sompuras / Raj Mistris who continue to build and care for buildings following traditions of their ancestors; Recognizing, too, the concept of jeernodharanam, the symbiotic relationship binding the tangible and intangible architectural heritage of India as one of the traditional philosophies underpinning conservation practice;

Noting the growing role of a trained cadre of conservation architects in India who are re-defining the meaning and boundaries of contemporary conservation practices; Convinced that it is necessary to value and conserve the unprotected architectural heritage and sites in India by formulating appropriate guidelines sympathetic to the contexts in which they are found;

We, members of INTACH, gathered here in New Delhi on the 4th day of November 2004, adopt the following Charter for Conservation of Unprotected Architectural Heritage and Sites in India.

4.3 Conclusion

In this chapter we have discussed about INTACH, the largest conservation related society in India.

Chapter 5: Overview of Architectural Styles in Ancient and Medieval India

In this chapter, we discuss some common architectural styles used in the construction of temples, mosques, palaces and other monuments in India during the ancient and medieval era.

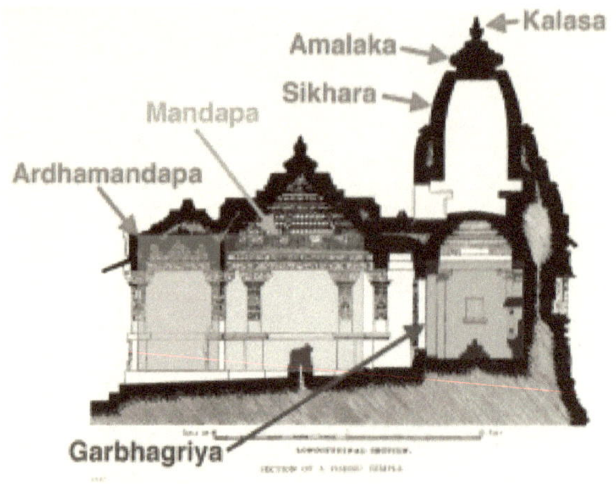

Figure: Elements of Hindu temple architecture in Nagara or North Indian style. Ms Sarah Welch, CC BY-SA 4.0 <https://creativecommons.org/ licenses/by-sa/4.0>, via Wikimedia Commons

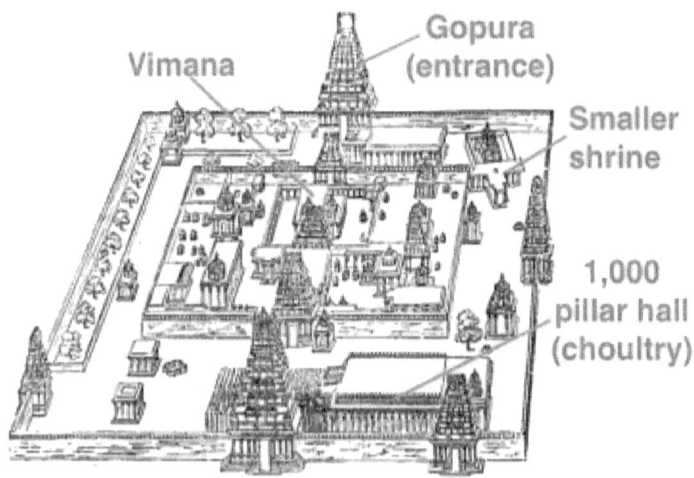

Temple at Tiruvallur (from Râm Râz's Essay on the Architecture of the Hindus).

Figure: Thirubvallur Tamil Hindu Temple Complex, built in typical Dravida style of temple architecture. E.B. Havell (1915), Public domain, via Wikimedia Commons

5.1 Principles of construction of Hindu temples in ancient india

In ancient India, the construction of Hindu temples followed certain principles taken from a scripture known as Vastu Shastra. These included things such as the orientation, geometry, proportion, symbolism and aesthetics. The shrine and main entrance are usually east facing. Use of geometric shapes such as circles and squares are common. The Garbha Gruha or womb chamber is the innermost sanctum where the idol of the deity is placed. The highest part of the temple is known as Shikhara, called Vimana in South Indian temples.

Often, locally available materials were used in the construction such as stone, wood, and metal. The temples were usually decorated with intricate carvings and sculptures.

The ancient and medieval Indian Hindu temples follow a few distinct architectural styles, discussed below:

Nagara or North Indian style temple architecture: Khajuraho temples are built in this style. In this style, temples had a Garbhagruha or inner sanctum containing the diety, which was located directly under the shikhara or the tallest tower. Often the temple was built on an Adhisthana or plinth or base platform, sometimes with stairs leading to the temple. Before reaching the Grabhagruha, the devotee had to pass through the entrance porch or Ardha Mandapa, following which they entered the Mantapa or congregational hall, before finally reaching the Garbhagruha. There was also often a path for circumambulation of the temple by devotees. There is typically no wall around the temple compound.

Dravida or South Indian style temple architecture: The Brihadeeshwara Shiva temple in Thanjavur, the Shiva temple at Chidambaram, Meenakshi temple in Madurai, Venkateshwara Balaji temple in Tirumala are built in this style of architecture. Here, there is often a high wall around the temple compound. The front of the temple has a tall Gopuram or entrance gateway, which could be high with many stories. The main temple tower is known as Vimana which is shaped like a stepped pyramid. There is often what is called a 1000 pillar hall in the temple complex that has many decorated pillars. Many smaller shrines are also typically part of the temple complex. The garbha gruha typically has idols of two fierce looking dwarapalas or doorkeepers who guard the deity. There is usually a stambha or pillar at the front of the temple. The temple complex also has a square shaped reservoir of water. The temple is usually on flat ground rather than a base platform as in Nagara style.

Kalinga or Odiya style of temple architecture: This is found in the Jagannath temple in Puri and the Lingaraja temple in Bhubaneshwar. It combines some elements of the Nagara style with Dravida style, as well as adding some unique elements of its own. It includes the entrance structure known as bhog mandir, followed by Nat Mandir, followed by Jagamohan and finally the Garbha Gruha.

Other styles: There are also features unique to temples from Bengal such as the terracotta temples of Bishnupur, Assamese temples such as Kamakhya temple in Guwahati, temples from western India and so on.

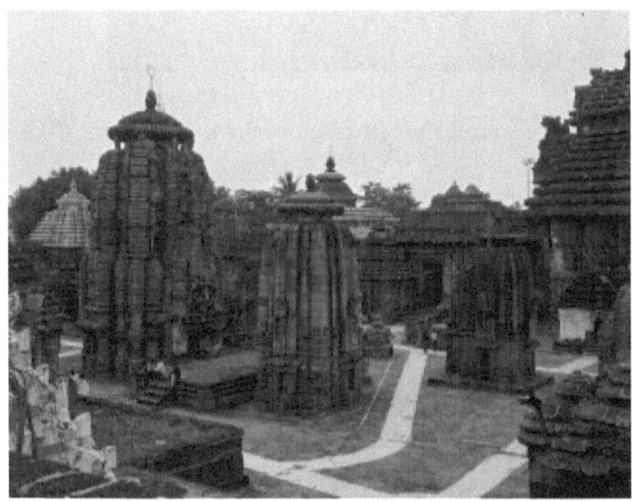

Figure: Lingaraja temple complex in Bhubaneshwar, built in Kalinga style. Photo taken by author.

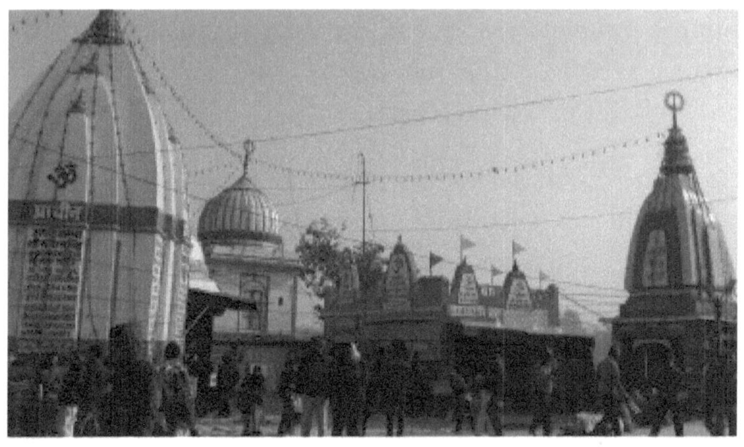

Figure: Ancient temples in Nagara style in Har ki Pauri, Haridwar. Photo taken by author.

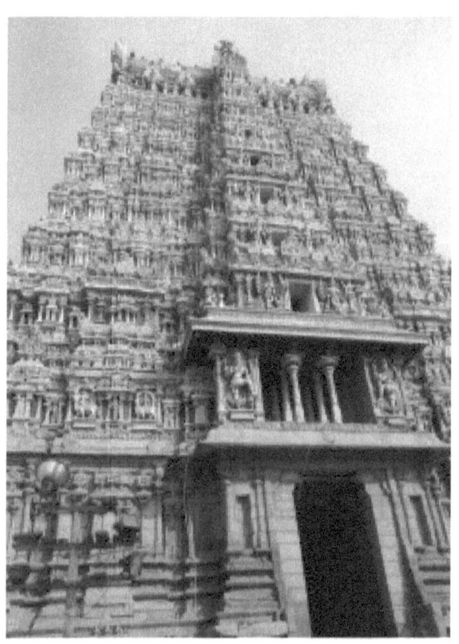

Figure: Gopuram of the Meenakshi temple in Madurai, built in Dravida style. Photo taken by author.

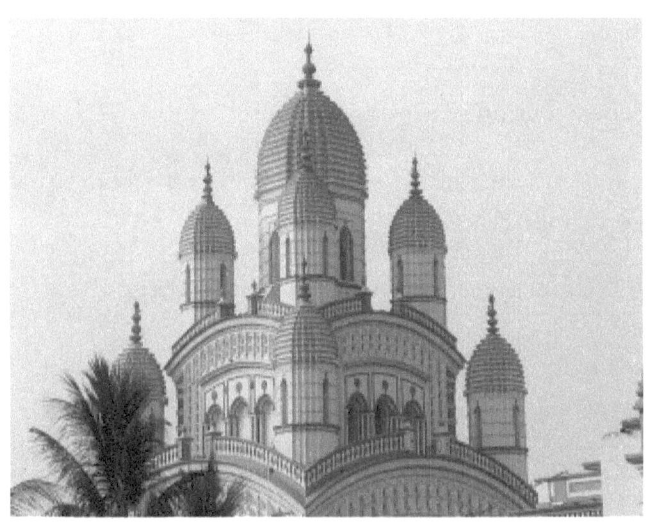

Figure: Dakshineshwar temple in Kolkata, built in Bengal style. Photo taken by author.

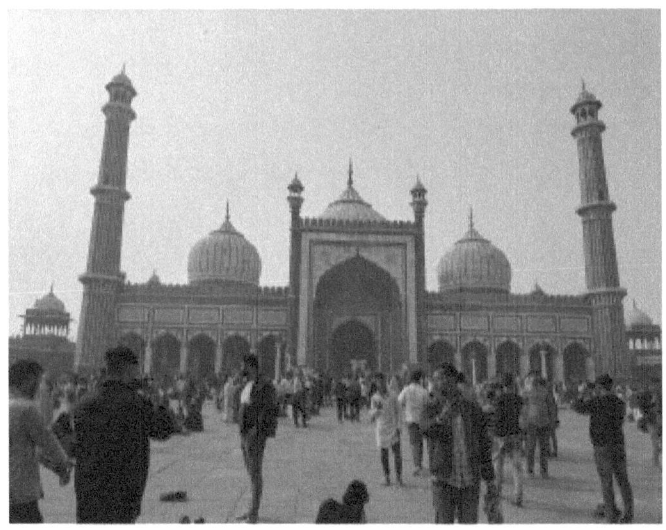

Figure: Jama Masjid in Delhi, built by the Mughal Emperor Shah Jahan in 17th century. Photo taken by author.

5.2 Principles of construction of mosques in India

Just like temples, mosques in India have a few common architectural elements and a few distinct styles.

The common architectural elements of mosques are as follows:

- It contains space for the congregation to offer namaz prayers, which may be an enclosed prayer hall or an open courtyard.
- It contains one or more minarets or tower from where the call to prayer is made five times a day.
- It has a water tank or taps with space for Wudu or washing feet ritual.
- The main building contains the Mihrab or a niche in the wall of the mosque that indicates the direction of Mecca, facing which the worshippers pray.
- There may be a small pulpit for the imam.
- It often (but not always) contains a dome, or in some cases 3 domes, which may be circular shaped or shaped like an onion bulb.
- There may be calligraphy of verses from the holy Quran on the walls or entrance.
- The walls of the mosque might be decorated with geometric patterns.
- They are built using materials such as brick, stone, and plaster, and often decorated with intricate tilework and carvings.
- The exterior of the mosque may consist of a main entrance and secondary entrances on the sides and cloisters surrounding the courtyard.

The earliest mosques in India date from the 12th -13th century Delhi sultanate era. These are typically simpler in structure and may not have fully formed domes. An example is the Quwwat Ul Mosque next to Qutub Minar in Delhi. Mosques during the Mughal empire adopted elements from a mixture of styles, including Persian, Arabic, central Asian and Hindu architecture. Awadh style, Deccan style, Shia style are all different unique styles of mosques in India.

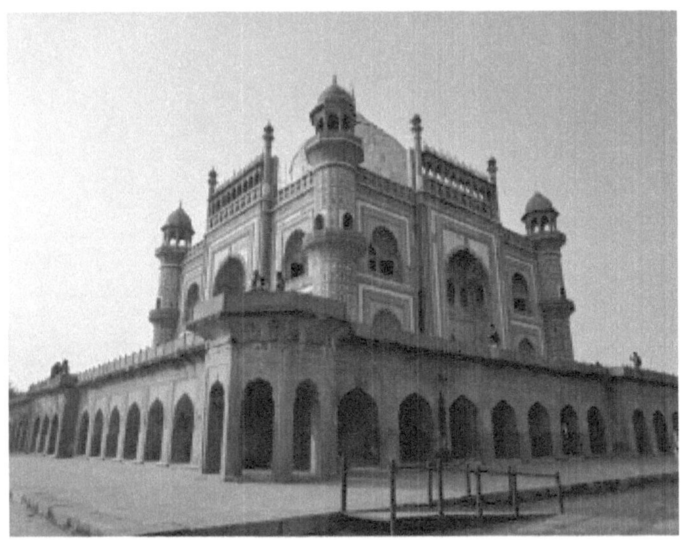

Figure: Safdarjung's tomb in Delhi, example of a medieval 17th century Islamic tomb in later Mughal style. Photo taken by author.

5.3 Islamic tombs in India

The layout of medieval Islamic tombs, such as Taj Mahal and Humayun's tomb has some common principles. It has the main building containing the main tomb (the grave of the main person, often along with graves of relatives of the main person) with decorated and grand arched entrances on all four sides, topped by a big circular or onion shaped dome and surrounded by Mughal gardens on all the four sides. As in mosques, the geometric patterns may adorn the walls. The building is usually square shaped and situated on a raised platform, symmetrical on each of the four sides. The construction materials can include marble and sandstone.

5.4 Conclusion

In this chapter, we have discussed a few principles of construction of ancient and medieval temples and mosques. Knowledge of such principles may be helpful in the reconstruction and conservation of these monuments.

Chapter 6: Techniques for Conservation of Monuments

In this chapter, we discuss some common techniques used in the conservation of monuments in India.

6.1 Ancient Vs Modern techniques for Conservation

Ancient techniques for conservation in India were based on traditional knowledge and materials, passed down through generations. These techniques included:

- **Use of traditional and locally available materials**: Traditional materials such as mud brick, lime mortar, and natural pigments were often used in construction of buildings in ancient India. Similarly, locally available materials were used to repair and maintain monuments and buildings, such as using sandstone, granite, and other types of rocks to repair and rebuild structures.

- **Climate control:** Buildings such as temple and forts in ancient and medieval India were often built to adapt to the local climate. This included elements of natural ventilation combined with shading and insulation to protect the interiors of the buildings and the people staying in them from the heat of the summers and high humidity.

Modern techniques for conservation in India are based on scientific principles and guidelines. These techniques include the following:

- **Use of modern materials**: Modern conservation work often use modern materials such as reinforced cement concrete, steel, and synthetic materials. Advanced technology such as laser scanning, 3D modeling, and remote sensing can also be used in the conservation and documentation of monuments and buildings.

- **Climate control**: Modern conservation involves the use of modern technology to control the internal climate of buildings and monuments, such as air-conditioning, heating, and ventilation systems.

6.2 Common techniques for conservation of buildings

The conservation of heritage monuments in India is a challenging task, as it involves preserving and protecting structures that are often centuries old, and which have historical, cultural, and architectural significance. Some of the more commonly used techniques for the conservation of heritage monuments in India include:

- **Preventive conservation**: This involves taking preventive measures to slow down the rate of deterioration of a monument, such as controlling the environment, pest management, and protection from weathering.
- **Structural stabilization**: This involves strengthening and stabilizing the existing structure of a monument to prevent further deterioration. This can be done with modern materials such as reinforced cement concrete or traditional materials such as mud and lime.
- **Preservation of original materials**: This involves preserving and protecting the original materials of a monument, such as stones, bricks, and plaster, to prevent further deterioration. This can be done using conservation-grade materials, such as lime mortar and natural pigments, during repairs and maintenance.
- **Cleaning and consolidation**: This involves cleaning and consolidating the surface of a monument to remove dirt, grime,

and other pollutants, as well as to strengthen the surface of the monument. This can be done using cleaning solutions and consolidating agents, such as lime and cement.

- **Climate control**: This can be done through the use of air conditioning and ventilation systems, as well as through the use of shading and insulation.
- **Restoration and reconstruction**: Restoration of damaged buildings to their original form can be done through the use of traditional materials and techniques, such as lime mortar.

6.3 Digital Technologies in Conservation

In recent years, digital technologies have transformed the field of heritage conservation, offering powerful new tools for documentation, analysis, and restoration planning. These technologies are increasingly being adopted in India alongside traditional conservation methods.

3D Laser Scanning and LiDAR: Terrestrial Laser Scanning (TLS) and LiDAR technology allow conservationists to create highly accurate, millimetre-precise three-dimensional point clouds of heritage structures without physical contact. These digital models serve as comprehensive records for conservation planning, detecting structural weaknesses such as micro-cracks or tilting, and guiding restoration work. They also enable the creation of virtual walkthroughs and immersive experiences for tourism. Projects in Uttar Pradesh, for example, have used TLS to document Nawabi-era palaces and temples in Lucknow and Varanasi, integrating the data into statewide digital heritage repositories. The Indian Digital Heritage (IDH) project, funded by the Department of Science and Technology, applied 3D laser scanning and computer vision at Hampi to digitally restore damaged sculptures, murals, and inscriptions, and to allow visitors to experience conjectural reconstructions of lost structures.

Artificial Intelligence and Machine Learning: Artificial intelligence (AI) tools, combined with high-resolution scanning and condition-monitoring sensors, are increasingly used to detect early signs of deterioration in monuments — including erosion, micro-cracks, and structural tilting — enabling proactive rather than reactive conservation. AI-powered platforms have been used at sites like the Elephanta Caves in Mumbai, where generative AI and 3D scanning were combined to recreate the 1,500-year-old UNESCO World Heritage site for virtual exploration, including interactive "Talking Tours" that explain the iconography of the ancient sculptures. Machine learning also assists in the analysis and classification of large archives of historic photographs and manuscripts.

National Mission on Monuments and Antiquities (NMMA): The National Mission on Monuments and Antiquities (NMMA), established in 2007, is spearheading the digitisation of India's vast built heritage. The mission has documented over 12.3 lakh antiquities and more than 11,400 heritage sites, establishing a unified national database. The NMMA has defined strict digital standards: built heritage and antiquities are photographed in uncompressed TIFF format at 300 dpi resolution. The companion initiative, Indian Heritage in Digital Space (IHDS), leverages modern digital technologies including 3D scanning, virtual reality, and artificial intelligence to create immersive experiences and research tools for both scholars and the general public. It also promotes crowdsourcing to build a collaborative digital heritage collection.

Drones and Remote Sensing: Unmanned Aerial Vehicles (drones) equipped with high-resolution cameras and LiDAR sensors enable rapid aerial surveys of large or difficult-to-access monument complexes. Remote sensing from satellites and drones can detect changes in site conditions, identify encroachments, and monitor the surrounding environment. The ASI, in collaboration with the Indian Space Research

Organisation (ISRO), has installed Automated Weather Stations (AWS) at several historical monuments to continuously monitor environmental factors such as wind speed, rainfall, temperature, and atmospheric pressure, enabling early detection of climate-related threats.

Virtual and Augmented Reality: Virtual reality (VR) and augmented reality (AR) technologies are increasingly used both as conservation tools and as means of public engagement. VR reconstructions of damaged or inaccessible monuments allow researchers to study ancient structures in detail without physical intervention. For the public, virtual tours of sites such as the Elephanta Caves and Hampi — available through platforms like Google Arts and Culture — make India's heritage accessible to audiences worldwide, reducing physical footfall pressure on fragile sites. The ASI has also created a portal, asimustsee.nic.in, showcasing nearly a hundred prominent monuments with panoramic views, historical information, and access details to promote heritage tourism.

6.4 Climate Change and Monument Conservation

Climate change has emerged as one of the gravest contemporary threats to India's built heritage. Rising temperatures, increasingly erratic monsoon rainfall, extreme weather events, rising sea levels, and intensified air pollution are accelerating the deterioration of monuments across the country at an alarming rate.

The effects are diverse and compounding. Rising temperatures and thermal fluctuations cause stone, brick, and mortar to expand and contract, leading to cracking and surface spalling. Intense humidity promotes algae, mould, and lichen growth on stone surfaces. Heavier monsoon rains cause flooding of subterranean archaeological sites and infiltrate foundations. Coastal monuments such as the Shore Temple in Mahabalipuram and the Konark Sun Temple in Odisha face accelerating salt corrosion and coastal erosion as sea levels creep higher. The walls of the 12th-century Sonar Fort in Jaisalmer partially collapsed due to heavy rainfall in August 2024, while a portion of the 600-year-old Nalagarh Fort in Himachal Pradesh had previously collapsed from rainfall, underscoring the urgency of the problem.

The ASI, in collaboration with ISRO, has set up Automated Weather Stations at key monuments to monitor environmental conditions in real time. Air Pollution Laboratories have been established at the Taj Mahal in Agra and Bibi Ka Maqbara in Aurangabad to track ambient pollutants. ASI officials participate in international workshops on disaster management of cultural heritage sites, organised in collaboration with UNESCO and the National Disaster Management Authority (NDMA). The NDMA and ASI have jointly developed National Disaster Management Guidelines for Cultural Heritage Sites and Precincts, covering risk assessment and emergency response protocols.

At the international level, the 46th session of the UNESCO World Heritage Committee, hosted by India at Bharat Mandapam in New Delhi in July 2024, highlighted the challenge of protecting heritage amid climate disruption. Indian Prime Minister Narendra Modi pledged one million US dollars at the session to support UNESCO's World Heritage Centre for conservation in India and across the Global South. Conservation experts increasingly argue that addressing climate change requires a fundamental shift in approach: from reactive repair to proactive climate adaptation, integrating scientific modelling of future climate scenarios into long-term preservation strategies for each monument.

6.5 Conclusion

In this chapter, we have discussed both traditional and modern techniques commonly used in the preservation and repair of buildings and monuments to save them from decay, as well as the growing role of digital technologies and the urgent challenge of climate change for monument conservation.

Chapter 7: Examples of Conservation of Monuments in India

In this chapter we discuss a few examples where work done by conservationists led by the Archeological survey of India has resulted in the repair and preservation of heritage monuments in India.

7.1 Humayun's Tomb in Delhi and surrounding areas

Humayun's Tomb in Delhi is a UNESCO World Heritage Site and an important example of Mughal architecture. The tomb underwent a major restoration project in the early 21st century, led by the Aga Khan Trust for Culture (AKTC) in partnership with the Archaeological Survey of India (ASI) and the Government of India.

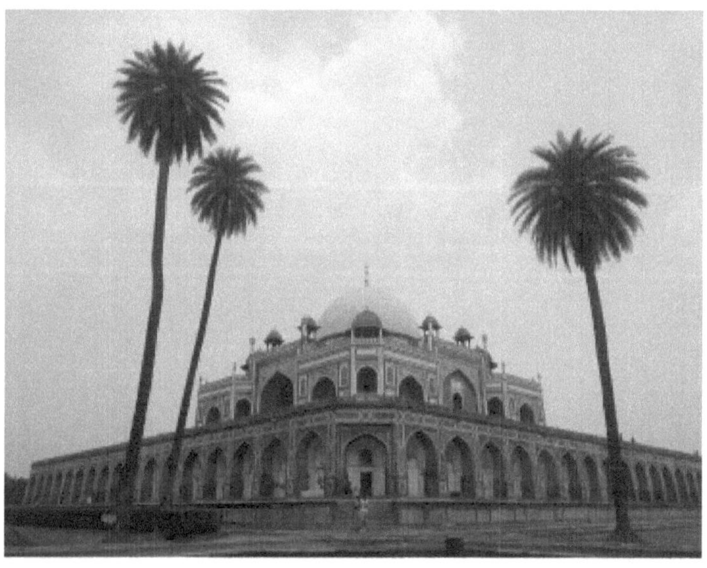

Figure: View of Humayun's tomb in Delhi. Photo taken by author

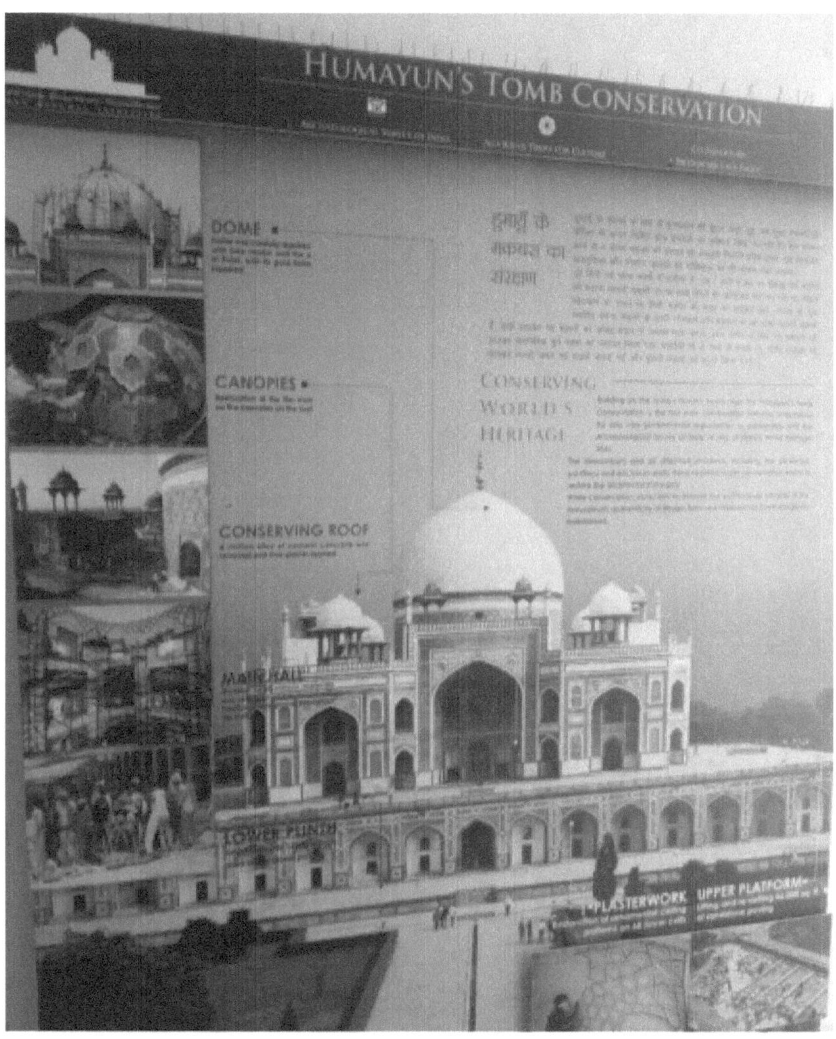

Figure: Poster about conservation work done on Humayun's tomb. Photo taken by author.

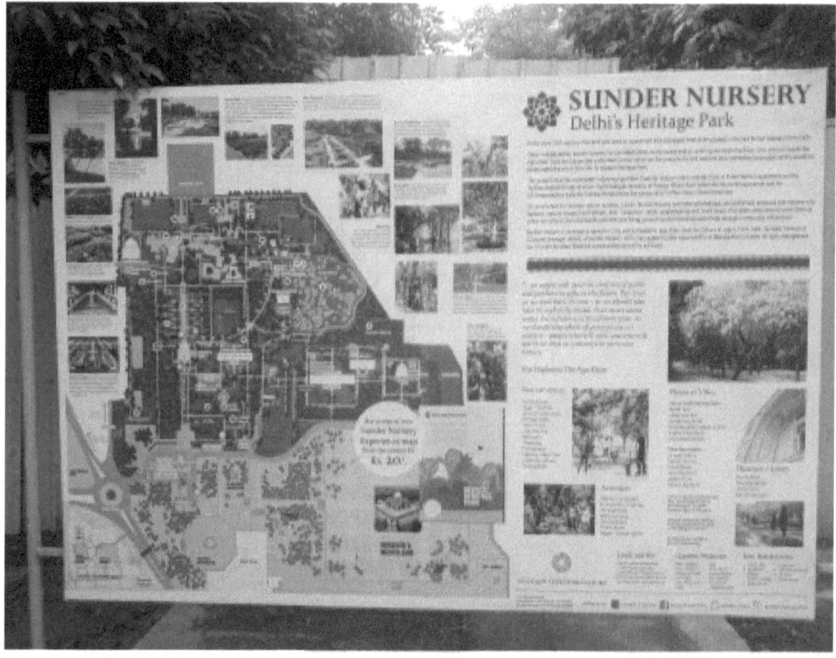

Figure: a poster about Sunder nursery, a park situated next to Humayun tomb filled with heritage monuments, maintained with funding from Aga Khan Trust. Photo taken by author.

The restoration project focused on the conservation and preservation of the tomb, as well as on the restoration of the garden and water features surrounding the tomb. The project had the components of structural stabilization using materials such as sandstone and lime mortar. The surface of the tomb was cleaned and consolidated. The garden and water features surrounding the tomb were restored to their original condition, based on historical records and research.

Also, the facilities in the Nizamuddin slum in surrounding areas of the tomb were improved and some of the people were gainfully employed in the preservation. Many of the important surrounding heritage structures that are not part of the Humayun's tomb complex were preserved by making a beautiful site called Sunder nursery filled with gardens and lush trees surrounding the heritage buildings.

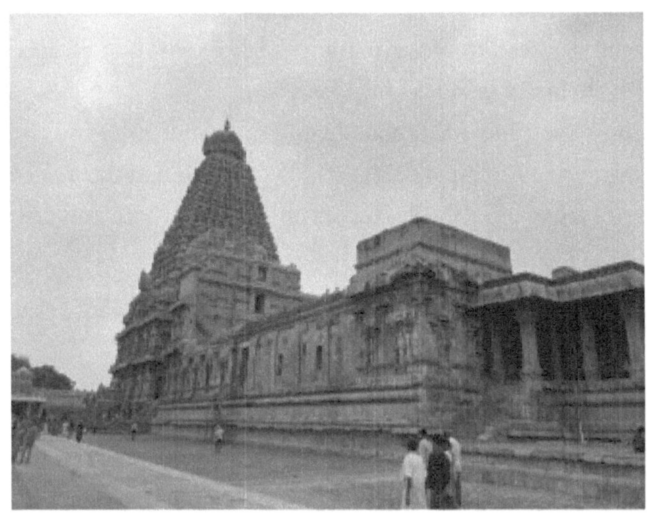

Figure: Chola big temple Brihadishwara in Thanjavur. Photo taken by author.

7.2 Chola Big Temple at Thanjavur

The Chola Big Temple, also known as the Brihadeesvara Temple, is a UNESCO World Heritage Site located in Thanjavur in Tamil Nadu. It is an excellent example of Chola architecture and was built by Rajaraja Chola in the 11th century.

The ASI repaired the temple over a number of years using various actions:

- One was clearing the site of encroachments such as a Veterinary hospital.
- Another was digging of the earth around the moat and the compound wall around the temple, which were almost buried to the ground floor level.

- Another was removal of some masonry walls from the Nayaka times.
- The surface of the main temple was cleaned of lichen and moss, then plaster was used to plug the joints and the surviving stucco work from the main building of the temple.
- For cleaning the lime wash coat from walls and pillars of the temple, modern cleaning materials such as diluted ammonia of 2% concentration were used after scrubbing with wire and coir brush.
- The smaller temples in the complex were also carefully restored.

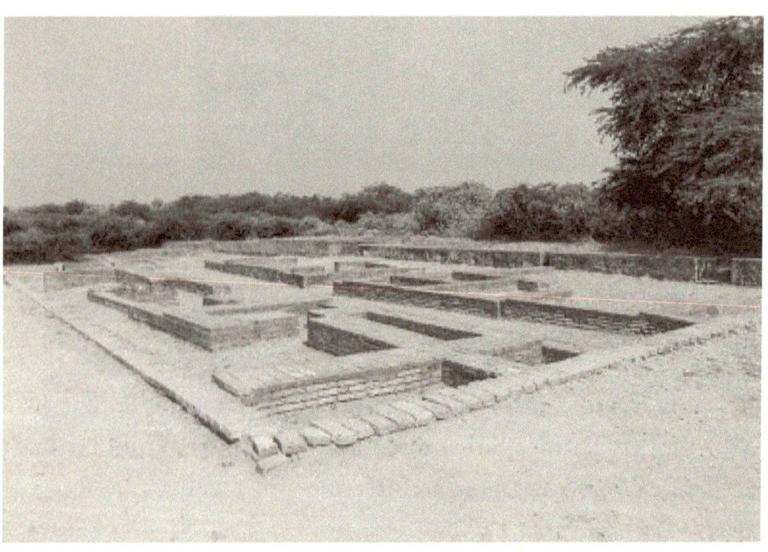

Figure: The lower town in the Lothal site of Indus valley civilization. Bernard Gagnon, CC BY-SA 3.0 <https://creativecommons.org/licenses/by-sa/3.0>, via Wikimedia Commons

7.3 Indus valley site in Lothal

The Indus Valley site in Lothal, located in Gujarat, India, is an important archaeological site that dates back to the Harappan civilization of the Indus Valley, which flourished around 2500 BCE. The site underwent a major restoration project in the 21st century, led by the Archaeological Survey of India (ASI).

The project focused on the conservation and preservation of the archaeological remains at the site, as well as on the restoration of the surrounding area. The project included elements such as excavation and documentation of the site to provide a better understanding of the layout and history of the site. The site was discovered relatively recently and so the restoration work is still ongoing.

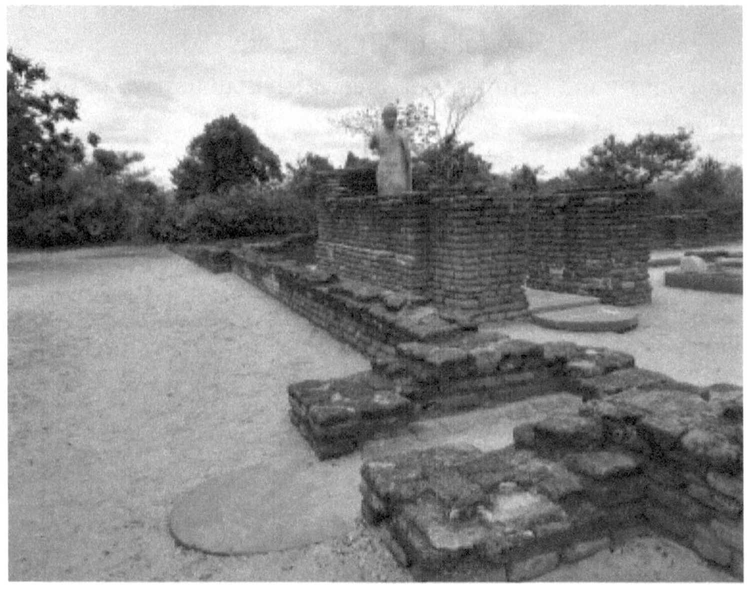

Figure: Transplanted Buddhist ruins in Nagarjunakonda island. Photo taken by author.

7.4 Transplantation of Nagarjunakonda site

Nagarjunakonda is an important archaeological site and Buddhist complex in Andhra Pradesh, from the Satvahanas of 3rd century AD. The site consists of several stupas, monasteries, and other structures.

However, the site was submerged under water due to the construction of the Nagarjunasagar Dam in the 1960s.

To preserve the cultural heritage of the site, the Indian government, in collaboration with UNESCO, decided to undertake an ambitious project of "transplantation" of the site before it got submerged. The site was mapped and replica structures were created using traditional materials and techniques. The replica structures were carefully transported and reconstructed on a nearby hilltop, above the water level, which was the new location of the site. While the transplantation project was able to preserve the physical remains of the site, it did not preserve the original context and setting of the site, which is an important aspect of any archaeological site.

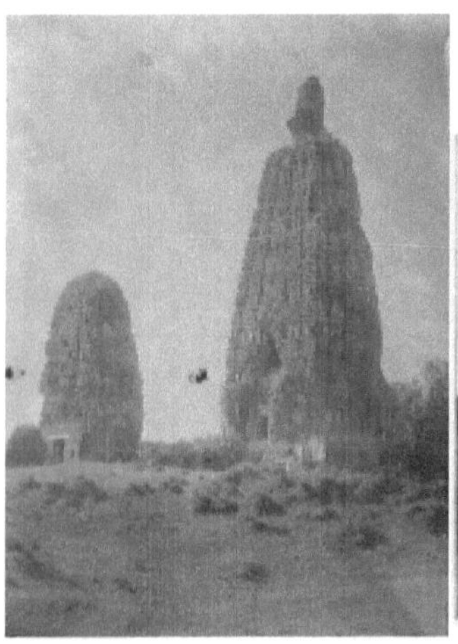
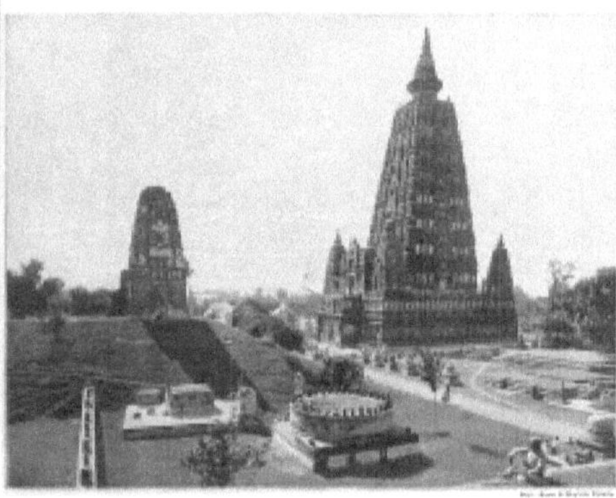

Figure: Mahabodhi temple in Bodhgaya before restoration and shortly after restoration in 1899. Public domain, via Wikimedia Commons

7.5 Early repairs to Mahabodhi temple

The Mahabodhi Temple, located in Bodh Gaya, India, is a UNESCO World Heritage Site and an important religious site for Buddhists. The temple underwent several repairs and renovations in the 19th century, as it had fallen into disrepair over the centuries.

One of the major repairs in the 19th century was led by Alexander Cunningham, a British archaeologist, who was appointed as the first Director-General of the Archaeological Survey of India (ASI). He led the restoration work between 1874 and 1885, which included reinforcing the structure, repairing the brickwork, and replacing the wooden beams with iron ones. Another major repair was led by Sir George Grierson, a British civil servant and linguist, who was appointed as the Superintendent of the Archaeological Survey of India (ASI) in 1902. He led the restoration work between 1902 and 1912, which included rebuilding the temple's spire, repairing the brickwork and the terracotta decoration, and restoring the statues and frescoes.

7.6 India's Conservation Work Abroad: Ta Prohm and My Son

India's expertise in monument conservation, built up over many decades by the ASI, has increasingly been extended to heritage sites beyond its borders, particularly in Southeast Asia, with which India shares deep historical and cultural ties rooted in the spread of Hinduism and Buddhism.

Ta Prohm Temple, Cambodia: In 2002, India signed an agreement with Cambodia for the restoration of the Ta Prohm temple complex, part of the famous Angkor Wat World Heritage Site. The temple, built by Khmer King Jayavarman VII between the 12th and 13th centuries CE, is known for its dramatic intertwining of massive tree roots with ancient stone structures. The ASI, working in association with the Cambodian authority for the protection of Angkor (APSARA), provided technical expertise, materials, and funding. Restoration of most of the complex was completed by 2012, including the placement of wooden walkways, platforms, and protective railings to shield structures from tourist footfall. In November 2022, the prestigious "Hall of

Dancers" at Ta Prohm was fully renovated and inaugurated by the Vice President of India. This project exemplified how India's conservation expertise and diplomatic relationships can be combined to protect shared global heritage.

My Son Cham Temples, Vietnam: ASI was also assigned the task of conserving and restoring three blocks of ancient Cham temples at My Son in Vietnam, a UNESCO World Heritage Site. Work began in 2017, with a team of Indian experts in archaeology, architecture, and engineering conducting meticulous research into the original Cham construction materials and techniques to ensure authenticity of the restoration. During the restoration work in 2020, the ASI team made a remarkable discovery: a monolithic sandstone Shiva linga dating to the 9th century CE. The restoration was completed in April 2023. These projects in Cambodia and Vietnam are a testament to India's growing role in global heritage conservation and reflect what Prime Minister Narendra Modi has described as a "civilizational connect" with India's extended neighborhood.

7.7 Conclusion

In this chapter we have considered a few examples where conservation and repairs of heritage sites have been performed in India, as well as examples of India's conservation work abroad, which underlines the country's growing role in global heritage preservation.

Chapter 8: Conclusion

In the previous chapters of this book, we have discussed some of the principles of conservation, the key international charters and declarations that guide conservation practice worldwide, organizations like the Archaeological Survey of India and INTACH dedicated to conservation of heritage monuments, the main architectural styles of ancient and medieval Indian monuments, as well as common conservation techniques — including the rapidly growing role of digital technologies such as 3D scanning, artificial intelligence, and virtual reality — and the urgent challenge posed by climate change. We have also looked at how the principles of conservation were applied to preserve and repair a number of heritage sites in India, as well as examples of India's conservation work abroad at sites such as Ta Prohm in Cambodia and My Son in Vietnam.

India's heritage landscape is also rapidly evolving. As of 2024, India has 43 UNESCO World Heritage Sites, with Charaideo Moidams in Assam being among the most recently inscribed. India hosted the 46th UNESCO World Heritage Committee in New Delhi in 2024, pledging one million US dollars to support UNESCO's World Heritage Centre for conservation globally. The Adopt a Heritage 2.0 programme is drawing corporate resources into monument upkeep, while the National Mission on Monuments and Antiquities is building a comprehensive digital archive of India's built heritage. These are encouraging signs of a broadening coalition of stakeholders — government, private sector, civil society, and international partners — committed to safeguarding India's cultural heritage.

Preservation of our shared heritage is the responsibility of all of us. Hence it is important to make it a priority and work together to play our part in preservation. For common citizens, this may involve learning about the factors that damage buildings and how they can be preserved, raising awareness and joining or helping NGOs such as INTACH that are dedicated to heritage preservation. Only if all of us work together can the glorious heritage of India be preserved for posterity.

About the authors

Siva Prasad Bose is an author of introductory guidebooks on aspects of Indian laws. He is currently retired after many years of service as an electrical engineer in Uttar Pradesh Power Corporation Limited. He received his engineering degree from Jadavpur University, Kolkata and has a law degree from Meerut University, Meerut and a BSc from MMH College, Ghaziabad. His interests lie in the fields of family law, civil law, law of contracts, and areas of law related to power electricity related issues. He lives in Delhi.

Joy Bose is a data scientist and author based in Bengaluru, India. He holds an LLM (Master of Laws) degree from Golden Gate University, San Francisco.

Other Books by Siva Prasad Bose

Introduction to Wills and Probate

Senior Citizens Abuse in India

Introduction to Negotiable Instruments

Introduction to Marriage Laws in India

Neighbor Problems in India and what to do about them

Delays in Court Cases in India

Self-Publish Books and E-Books in India

Introduction to Patents and Patent Law in India

Introduction to Property Law in India

Did you love *Introduction to Conservation of Indian Monuments*? Then you should read *Historical Cities of Delhi: Walks Using the Delhi Metro*[1] by Siva Prasad Bose and Joy Bose!

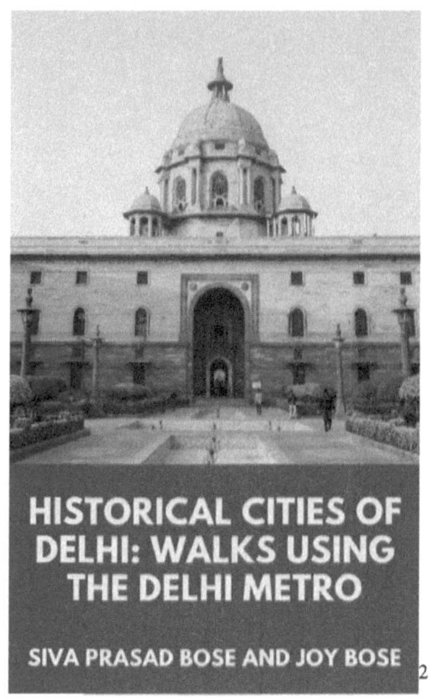

[2]

Delhi is much more than just the capital of India. It is a city with an amazing history. So many times, it has been the major city or capital of India, from the earliest Mahabharata days to the Rajputs to the Delhi Sultanate to the Mughals to the British. Each time the new rulers left their mark on the city. As a result, now we have a Delhi which has the mark of at least seven or eight different historical cities, if not more.

In this book, we review the different historical cities of Delhi. We use the Delhi metro, which is currently probably the best developed metro in India, as the preferred means of transport to see the sights of the seven

---

1. https://books2read.com/u/31DLKl

2. https://books2read.com/u/31DLKl

cities of Delhi. We hope that this short guide will help the reader the experience a little bit of what Delhi is all about, its people and its history.

In this book, we do not cover all the historical sites or attractions of Delhi, such as the many modern museums, markets and other attractions. Rather, we focus on the sites that form part of the historical cities of Delhi and those that are located within the historical boundaries of those cities.

This book was born out of many travels and exploratory walks made by the authors in Delhi, where they live.

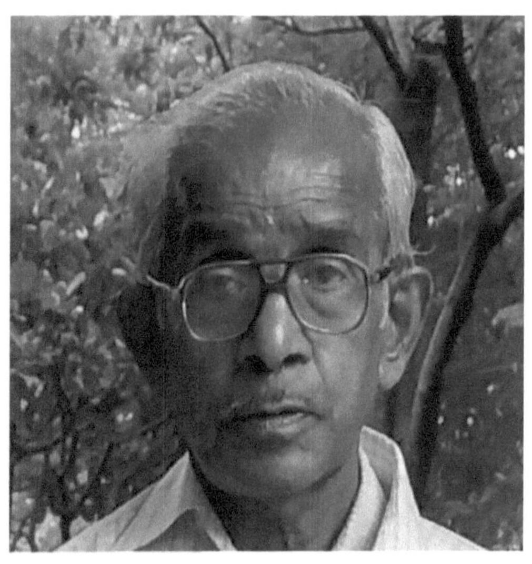

About the Author

Siva Prasad Bose is an electrical engineer by profession. He is currently retired after many years of service in Uttar Pradesh Power Corporation Limited. He received his engineering degree from Jadavpur University, Kolkata and has a law degree from Meerut University, Meerut. His interests lie in the fields of family law, civil law, law of contracts, and any areas of law related to power electricity related issues.

Read more at https://sivaprasadbose.wordpress.com/.